W9-DIH-753

I Love You, Granny

A GRANDMOTHER'S FIRST HANDBOOK

Betty Locke

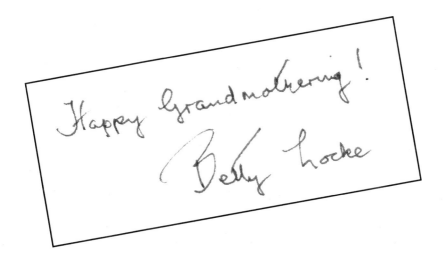

Happy Grandmothering!

Betty Locke

Vanwell Publishing Limited
St. Catharines, Ontario

Design: Linda Moroz-Irvine
Vanwell Publishing Limited
1 Northrup Crescent
P.O. Box 2131
St. Catharines, Ontario L2R 7S2
sales@vanwell.com
phone 800.661.6136
fax 905.937.1760

Printed in Canada

Library and Archives Canada Cataloguing in Publication

Locke, Betty, 1917-
    I love you, Granny / Betty Locke.

ISBN 978-1-55125-137-0

1. Grandmothers. 2. Grandmothers--Family relationships.
I. Title.

HQ759.9.L63 2008   306.874'5   C2008-905694-9

To my sons, their wives and my grandchildren whose
support and inspiration helped me immeasurably
in the writing of this book.

Contents

The 2nd edition of this book is offered by the
NYANYAS OF NIAGARA
For the benefit of
THE STEPHEN LEWIS FOUNDATION'S
GRANDMOTHERS TO GRANDMOTHERS CAMPAIGN

THE STEPHEN LEWIS FOUNDATION (SLF) helps to ease the pain of HIV/AIDS in Africa by funding well over 140 community-level initiatives that provide care and support to women, orphans, grandmothers and people living with HIV/AIDS in 15 sub-Saharan African countries.

In March of 2006 the Foundation launched a Grandmothers to Grandmothers Campaign which seeks to raise awareness and mobilize support in Canada for Africa's grandmothers. These heroic women bury their own children who have died from HIV/AIDS and then look after their bereaved grandchildren.

Since the launch of the Grandmothers to Grandmothers Campaign, over 200 groups of Canadian grandmothers and "grand others" have taken up the call to action and the Campaign has raised over $4 million. The SLF directs these funds to community level organizations that provide African grandmothers with much needed support; including housing grants, food, school fees and grief counselling for themselves and their grandchildren.

Our local grandmother group is the Nyanyas of Niagara. Nyanya means grandmother in Swahili. The group was officially formed in Niagara-on-the-Lake in the fall of 2007 by a handful of enthusiastic women. At the time of this printing the membership has expanded to over 90 ladies throughout the Niagara Region!

We are all committed, in various ways, to raising money for the SLF and the Grandmothers to Grandmothers Campaign. Our second major fun(d)raiser is this book of heart-warming, practical and humorous advice to "new" grandmothers.

An enormous hug and thank you goes to Betty Locke and her family for providing us with the opportunity to share her insight, warmth and wisdom on this important stage in a woman's life.

For more information on the Stephen Lewis Foundation and the Grandmothers to Grandmothers Campaign, please visit
www.stephenlewisfoundation.org,
email: campaign@stephenlewisfoundation.org
or call: 1-416-533-9292 or 1-888-203-9990.

Introduction

IT WOULD SEEM that everyone has a book written for them these days. Browsing through a bookstore, I saw books for the overweight, the overwrought, and the oversexed. Troubled teens, frantic feminists, muddled middle-agers and recalcitrant retirees can all find books that speak to their needs. But where was a book for graying grandmothers, particularly those who are the mothers of baby boomers and now grandmothers of their progeny? Caught between the old traditional values of their upbringing and the broad social changes being experienced by this generation, these grandmothers face the challenge of re-defining their role. To help them do this was my reason for writing this book.

It would be presumptuous to assume that I had all the answers on how to be a great, or even a good, grandmother. Yet I firmly believe that the answers were out there somewhere. To find them, I delved into the minds and hearts of hundreds of grandmothers and grandchildren in North America. The result is not a sociological treatise nor yet a simplistic "How To" book. Instead it reflects the wisdom and wonder of grandmothers like myself and grandchildren like my own.

It is my fervent hope that those grandmothers who read this book will find it entertaining, informative and even inspirational. Should they successfully re-define or enhance their grandmotherly role, their supreme accolade may well be to hear that one simple statement, "I Love You, Granny."

Foreword

AS I WRITE THIS in the winter of 2008, my mother, Janet E. (Betty) Locke is now in a retirement home at the age of 91. She has a form of dementia that comes with her advancing years. Her active days are behind her, but she still retains her feisty manner and is determined to get "out and about" when the weather gets better. We'll see. But knowing Betty as I do, anything is possible.

In this last year, Betty has graduated from Granny to Great Granny, with the birth of my grandson, James Ryan Lindsay. She is always delighted to see him and they seem to share a language all of their own. She enjoys his loving nature and quite proudly considers him "so cute".

Betty was brought up in a strict environment in Montreal. Her first 2 years of school were difficult as she was forced to write right-handed and it took her a while to get used to it. From that beginning, she went on to be an excellent student and graduated from McGill in the '30's, when not many young ladies were going to university. Years as an accomplished English teacher along with extensive worldwide work with the Brownie movement, gave her great satisfaction in the professional side of her life. It also gave her children and grandchildren a fine example to follow.

But of relevance to this foreword was the strong role Betty played in bringing up her two sons, my younger brother Donald and I. My father was not well (he was quite a bit older than Betty) and she had to do most of the parenting herself. We always felt we could count on mother for love, support and encouragement. We were very privileged to have such an excellent mother, but probably didn't appreciate it at the time. As the years go by, we realize how fortunate we were.

Next came the grandchildren… and they all helped us celebrate a great birthday party we had for Granny when she turned 90. Among other things, each grandchild wrote a note about their special memories with Granny, and below are some excerpts:

Sarah – "doing morning exercises and getting "scratchy scratchies" in your bed when you visited; learned from you a passion for the arts"

Jessica – "such a positive impact on the lives around you; blessed to have you in my life"

Lauren – "constant inspiration and touchstone taught me to appreciate reading and gave me an appetite for travel"

Peter – "you have defined us, the entire Locke family; your legendary competitiveness in games like Scrabble"

Charlie – "story telling in bed with no books, just imagination and free thought; the sense of peacefulness, safety and comfort obtained from the unbridled love from my Granny"

Of course, every note also expressed their love and affection for their Granny. And maybe this wonderful relationship that Betty had with her grandchildren was the motivation behind the writing of this book.

This book came when Betty was in her 70's. She said she would like to do something with her spare time. I suggested she write a book about grandparenting and she agreed! We published 2500 copies of the first edition and Betty sold all of them herself. She gave talks about art appreciation and about the new National Gallery in Ottawa (where she lived then). At the end of the presentation she gave a short spiel on her book and signed copies for those who bought one.

As you can tell, we feel Betty is a very special person and we are very fortunate to have her. This makes the decision to help out the Stephen Lewis Foundation's Grandmothers to Grandmothers Campaign a "no-brainer". Who would not want to assist the grandmothers in Africa to care for their ill adult children and bereaved grandchildren? When approached about this possibility, Betty was very touched and delighted that her book will be used to help other less fortunate grandmothers and their loved ones.

Betty's family truly feels the positive sentiments towards grandparents as expressed in this book. WE LOVE YOU, GRANNY.

Stephen Locke

This is you, Granny.

This is me.

J.L.

Chapter 1

What Are Grandmothers Made Of?

Grandparents are like parents...
only more Grander. Dale Greeting Card

THE NURSERY RHYME tells what little girls and boys are made of. To ascertain what grandmothers are made of necessitated some intense research. Surveys were sent to grandmothers all over this continent. Interviews were held with countless grandchildren in Ottawa schools. Newspaper and magazine articles were closely read for some understanding of this special person. For special you are, if one can believe the many youngsters who stated this was so. What, then, makes you so special?

The physical aspect of a grandmother should be a starting point.

When I first became a grandma a dozen years ago, a dear friend sent me a brilliant article by Sheila Keiran called "On Sharing Your World". The author gave me some tremendous insights about this new relationship and quite likely, was the source of inspiration for this book. She wittily wrote, "Of television's grandparents the less said the better; they may be described as a set of false teeth and a whine connected by a cranky digestive tract to fat, lisle-stockinged legs."

It was not surprising that most grandchildren agreed that Granny was old; some even mentioned wrinkles, glasses, gray hair, and funny clothes. Superfluous avoirdupois was obliquely described in the words "fat and loveable". When one grandma commented on her extra weight, Kathy (Age 6) consoled her with, "That's all right. Grandmothers are supposed to be fat." Another plump granny, wondering whether the grandchildren would grow up tall and slim, like her son was reassured by Jennifer (Age 3), "Never mind, Grandma, I'll stay short and fat, just like you." I can recall the exquisite tact of Sean (Age 4) as he watched me gardening, clad comfortably but unbecomingly in shorts. Said he, "I see some big knees out here." A much-quoted essay, purportedly written some years ago by an eight-year old, stated, "Usually they are fat but not too fat to tie a kid's shoes. They wear glasses and funny underwear. They can take their teeth and gums off."

In all fairness one must acknowledge that many grandmothers today are slim and trim. They dress fashionably and have their own teeth and may even wear contact lenses and dye their hair. But confronted by such stereotypical views in press and TV showing grandmothers as physically unattractive and emotionally stunted, it was a relief to turn to my surveys and see in what high esteem grandmothers held themselves.

When asked how they rated themselves as grandparents, 40% replied very good and 23% the best! Having a good relationship with their grandchildren was considered important by 83%. Their answers to the question about what is really great about being a grandmother revealed much emotional health and a clear understanding of what is really special about grandmothering.

The responses of the many young children I interviewed in their classrooms were also reassuring. When I asked them to complete this statement: Grandmothers are _____ the words most frequently used were: nice, caring, loveable, good, special, great, loving, sweet and fun. So, dear grandmothers, you are not the caricatures of press and media.

You do have intellectual curiosity about your role. You look honestly at the rewards and drawbacks of being a grandmother. You are eager to foster a loving relationship with your grandchild which, like any relationship, takes time and energy. The ensuing chapters are written to show you some ways to expend that time and energy.

Who knows, you may even be able to become a grandmother like the Queen Mother who was described by her grandson, Prince Charles, as "the most wonderful example of fun, laughter, warmth, infinite security and, above all, exquisite taste."

For special you are, if one can believe the many youngsters who stated this was so...

My grandmother loves me and that's why I love her.
– Grade 5 pupil

My Nanny is very special to me and she is very kind.
– Grade 5 pupil

My grandma is loving and concerned about me.
– Grade 6 pupil

My grandmother was giving, tender, loving and considerate.
– Grade 6 pupil

My grandmas love me so much I can't tell the difference between them.
– Grade 6 pupil

I love my grandmother. I think she is the best. She is always concerned about me and my friends. She has a heart of gold.
– Grade 4 pupil

My grandmother died. I never saw her ever once but I know she's beautiful.
– Grade 3 pupil

On a personal note

Echoing the sentiments on a Birthday card she had sent me, my granddaughter wrote in her newly-acquired cursive writing:

You listen and you understand.
It's true, times spent with you are special to me.
And I treasure you.

Chapter 2
Beatific
Beginnings

THE SHEER OPTIMISM with which parents view that moment when they will be alone with their first-born is a condition common to all such innocents. It is for grandmothers and experienced parents to realize that this may well be the most stress-filled, frustrating and exhausting period in their lives.

If you are the mother of the new mother, you are usually the first asked to offer yourself for duty during that traumatic time. Mothers of new fathers hover in the background waiting to take over when the other has served her stint.

Though much has been written about the impact of a new baby upon the young couple, has anything ever been written about the impact upon you, the neophyte grandmother?

As an experienced mother, you are considered an expert in the caring for this small scrap of humanity. They are convinced that you must know how to soothe their colicky baby. Now this is apt to be the first and last time that they will look upon you as an expert. It is very likely that their bed-side table is laden with all manner of baby books doling out the latest in baby lore. Once the new parents find the time and energy to read these books, your methods of baby-raising will instantly become suspect.

What if they should discover that twenty or thirty or more years ago you faced parenthood with a copy of Dr. Spock's book, a pile of the new rectangular cloth diapers and sex-coded pins (pink or blue guards) as your chief aids in baby care?

So, should you have a background similar to mine, perhaps you will agree that a refresher course in some aspects of baby care is a must. Let us tackle one end at a time.

Diapers

The commercials on TV must surely have convinced you that cloth diapers are a thing of the past. No self-respecting mother could possibly use a diaper that dripped, slipped or was not sufficiently absorbent.

This makes your hard-won expertise in washing, folding and pinning cloth diapers a lost art. It is up to you to learn the intricacies of the new plastic ones with the sticky strips to hold them on and the contoured backs and fronts for the perfect fit. I have been known to reduce the fastening strips to non-sticking shreds in an effort to place the diaper tightly around a squirming infant – the surreptitious use of a safety-pin filled me with guilt.

I have just discovered that a strip that can be used over and over has been introduced by a kindly manufacturer. You will also be happy to learn that the treatment of used diapers is no longer the unmentionable task of our era. You just fold them up and pitch them out.

All in all these modern diapers deserve any sane grandmother's seal of approval.

Feeding

Here, too, you face another adjustment. The chances are excellent that your grandchild will be breast-fed. That this was not always so in our time is evident by those haunting memories of sterilizers, glass bottles, bottle-brushes, funnels and the odour of rubber nipples boiling on the stove.

Enough of these ghosts of yesteryear. Today's emphasis on breast-feeding is to be commended. Your encouragement and support of the new mother in this endeavour can be your best gift to her and your new grandchild.

It is, of course, possible that some babies will still be bottle-fed or that supplementary bottles must be given. If so, take heart. Plastic bottles with their sterile liners are a cinch to use once you have mastered the art of their assembly. Though touted to be free of air, these bottles do not do away with that time-honoured activity of baby-burping. It will be found that grandmother's hand has not lost its cunning. You will still be the one best able to produce resounding burps and dribbling smiles from that milk-sated infant.

The frequency of feeding these days depends on demand. How sensible! Remember how we were told to feed our babies at set times only? Consistency was the watchword. I quote from a yellowed clipping dated from the 1940's:

"Dr. W.E. Blatz, Director of the Institute of Child Study of the University of Toronto, advocates that babies be permitted to cry it out instead of being fed or otherwise placated."

"Since it is obvious that the child has to be frustrated some time in life, the sooner it happens the better,' Dr. Blatz declared. 'It becomes as part of a routine… following a principle that consistency in training is more important than love,"

This evoked a stinging response in a poem written by Mary Lowery Ross of which I quote the final stanza:

> So cry, my Child. No interference
> Will come from your devoted parents,
> However piteously you beseech them.

You must cross frustrations
Before you reach them.
Although your pain with anguish fills me,
I'll be consistent if kills me,
And sternly sever the Silver Cord
So you'll grow up brave and strong and probably
horrid.

I'm grateful that my grandchildren experienced their babyhood in more compassionate times.

How should the new grandma fit in on this first important visit?

First be thankful for the strides made in baby care. Accept these enlightened changes gladly. Then remember that your moral support to the parents, your experienced hand in the laundry and kitchen, and your offer to take an early morning supplementary feeding will be the small price you have to pay for the absolute delight of holding once again a small baby and feeling its feathery hair against your cheek.

Haiku for My Grandchildren

Baby's tiny fist
Captures my heart and finger
In its tender twist
J.E.L.

Diapering – the Way it Was

If you enjoy Spoonerisms, read aloud this gem which Colonel Stoopnagle wrote for the *Saturday Evening Post*,

How to Bainge a Daiby's Chyper

Nesibgreedy Insairients
Baby, Dightly slamp
Diaper. Drean and Cly
Paifty Sins   Palcum Towder
Pots of Laishunce

When the baby criaby byes, crift him gently from the lib and shay him carefully over your loalder, delly-bown. Rawk, do not won, to the bathroom and bay the laiby down on a blawft sanket. Recloove his moathes until he is nactically praikid – until nothing remains but the baby and the dett wiaper.

Now, undo the draifty sins, and holding the strower exlemities aloft by raising his legs and fegs, deel off the used pyper and sauce it atide. Select a nice dean clyper (the roddern one are mectangular) and tatter plenty of scalsum on both viper and dictim. Mold both ends of the diaper towards the fiddle, one a fet-tle larther than the other, porming a sort of fannel for more sorpisfactory ab-sat-shun. Elevate the raiby's beer and pull one end (of the chyper not the dialed) between the lugster's yeggs, and pin it at each side of the hittle one's lips.

If the crild chize after all this bunkey mizzness, mertinly it isn't because he's soist – he either botts his wantle or his little elly bakes.

In A Much More Serious Vein

I pass on this excerpt from an article in the Chatelaine maga-zine. Though addressed to the new mother, it has much of value to say to the new grandmother.

British sociologist Ann Oakley, in a 1979 study of first-time mothers, found that close to three-quarters of her 66 subjects had received practical help from their mothers after birth. For many new moms, this support helped to ward off loneliness and depression.

The catch is that the new grandmother's emotions may be almost as mixed as her daughter's. Even the most lovable grandchild reminds a woman of her advancing years and lost fertility. Indeed, the birth may coincide with other reminders, such as the death of a spouse.

The myth of all-knowing self-sacrificing motherhood can compound the new grandmother's unease. "Most new grandmothers are absolutely terrified that they didn't train their daughters well enough for motherhood," says Dr. Paula Caplan, a psychologist at the Ontario Institute for Studies in Education in Toronto. "So they try to do more training right on the spot."

A frequent result is arguments over child care. The mother may want to breast-feed on demand, while the grandmother insists that the new mom will spoil the baby unless she follows a schedule. If the new father tries to be a peacekeeper, his wife may enlist him as an ally. The grandmother understandably concludes that they do not value her support.

A little planning goes far towards preventing such clashes:

- Consider the timing. If you and your mother have been bickering for years, an immediate extended visit spells trouble. You might tell her, "We'd love to see you once we get to know our new baby."

- Tell your mother how she can help you. Should she cook the meals, leaving the baby to you? Or do you want her to take care of the baby while you rest? Keep your expectations reasonable: some first-time grandmothers who have not looked after infants in years feel as awkward with newborns as do first-time mothers.

- Share your mother's memories of becoming a mother. Chances are you've already heard part of her story. But you may not know your mother's first impressions of you, how your father responded to parenthood or how she recalls her own mother's first meeting with you. The more you treat each other like caring friends, the better the outlook for a successful first visit.

- Think positively. Dr. Stewart says that some women interpret a mother's innocent comment, "Maybe the baby needs burping" as an implied criticism. They expect their mothers to pass judgement on their child-rearing abilities, but this feeling is a relic of their former dependent status as little girls. Similarly, fear of offending her formerly all-powerful mother can prevent a new mom from raising a legitimate concern. If your mother's anxious hovering over your baby's crib is making you nervous, tell her so.

- Show your appreciation. Your mother may be abandoning a job, a husband, or a volunteer commitment to help you and your family. But meeting your needs is no longer her responsibility. Like any devoted friend, she deserves a gift – perhaps flowers or a new best seller, to help her relax when she goes home.

Rona Maynard

Chapter 3
Visiting Privileges

SINCE THE SURVEYS REVEAL that most grandmothers today do not live with grandchildren, the question of visiting becomes an extremely important factor in the grandmother-grandchild relationship. A few ground rules about visiting and being visited should be helpful.

Visiting

The very obvious courtesies which you extend in visiting friends should apply to visiting your sons and daughters. Just as you would not think of dropping in on friends without a previous phone call, so should you give your children the opportunity of knowing your plans. If you are visiting from afar, your arrival and departure dates should be discussed and be mutually agreeable.

These rules are elementary, you may scoff, but you would be surprised at the lack of communication which often exists between the generations. Some grandmothers wail that they are never invited to visit; others bemoan the fact that they are never invited except as an afterthought or as a baby sitter. I would be the last to deny that such situations do exist. But this book is about grandmothering and the focus must remain on visiting rules which will enhance your visit for both you and your grandchildren.

Let us first consider the visit from a distance. As you are the guest you will fit quickly and comfortably into the daily routine. No demands for early morning tea or special attention should even be considered.

Most grandmothers' wake early and I've found this is a glorious time to enjoy my young grandchildren. I invite them to visit my bed for these early morning cuddles and confidences. I usually restrict their entrance into my room to seven o'clock. This they understand when I explain that I am old and need my rest. The latter is also a valid excuse for a two hour rest in the afternoon, when reading, snoozing and letter writing will take you out of circulation and help you recharge your batteries for the activities you have planned. Yes, come on your visit with some ideas for things to do with the kids. Ask them for ideas too. Walks, visits to parks, museums, restaurants or the theatre may seem prosaic, but ways of making them memorable will be discussed in a later chapter.

Visiting during the school year has a built-in benefit. Maybe you are on hand for that quality time when the grandchildren return from school eager for a grandmother's attention. (Also, you do not have to play second fiddle to Santa Claus, the Easter Bunny or a pile of birthday presents.)

For the grandmother who lives near her children, the temptation to drop in may be very strong. You are particularly blessed if this behaviour is encouraged. It most cases a phone call is a must, even if only to find out if someone will be at home to welcome you.

If your visit is primarily to exchange views or news with the adults, inform the children of this and promise to talk to them later. Never hesitate to level with them; it is ignoring them completely which children resent.

If, however, you are there to dote on your grandchildren, do it honestly and wholeheartedly. Listen to their answers to your questions and above all, try to make your conversation with them interesting. One child complained, "She always asks me how I'm doing at school," another "She always says how tall I've grown."

Surely we can do better than that. Try "What interesting things have you been doing lately?" or "Stand with your back to me and see how soon you'll be as tall as grandma." A warning here about endlessly discussing your physical ailments. This will not only turn off your whole listening audience, but also places a burden of worry upon a sensitive grandchild.

In "Beatific Beginnings" I have written at length about visiting that first wonderful grandchild. How about the arrival of subsequent grandchildren? It may be superfluous to even discuss this visit, but since this is a grandmother's first handbook, I think it should be mentioned.

When another child is born, gifts and attention are showered upon it. Did you ever observe the look on the 3-year old's face as visitors rush past her to coo over the new baby brother and present gifts to his mother? It would move the hardest heart.

All that is needed is your usual warm greeting and a "Would you show me your new baby brother?" This could be followed by presenting a small gift to the older child and by asking her assistance in unwrapping the present you have brought for the new baby. A jealous older child, when robbed of the attention formerly enjoyed, is very vulnerable.

Being Visited

GRANDMA
We've been thinking about you because it's
MOTHER'S DAY
You play with us,
You feed us good stuff

You don't yell,
You let us stay up late.

We've decided to move in with you.

Boynton Greeting Card

Here you are on firm ground. It is your home. You are in control. You can set the rules. It is in your power to set the scene for a satisfying visit for both you and your grandchildren.

This begins by recognizing your own limitations. For example, if you are in poor health, short visits are indicated.

If you are a fussy housekeeper, don't serve your grandchildren ice cream and cake in your beautifully appointed living room – seating them around the kitchen table, on the patio or on the floor of the family room will meet with their approval.

If you are an avid collector, don't expect a toddler to keep his hands off your cherished figurines. It has been said that an active two-year old should be able to touch 75% of the things in a room. So unless you enjoy a conversation that is limited to "No, No, No's" or watching a young mother's nerves being shredded into ribbons, relegate those collectibles to high places or out of sight altogether.

Unless you have the children to yourself, you must have free time for their parents. After all, family visits are enhanced by touching bases with them, learning of their views, their aspirations, their exploits and their news. So a supply of toys, books and games for the young ones would seem the obvious answer. One grandmother has a box of toys which belonged to her own children; and her grandchildren head for these as avidly as we would to artifacts in the Museum of Civilization.

When I want quiet conversation with my adult children, I see no harm in letting the grandchildren eat separately from us – a picnic on the lawn or plates in front of the TV is often much more suited to their wriggling forms. Most of the time, however, your whole family should have a welcome place at your table. Saying grace, listening to adult conversation and participating in family banter is a wonderful part of any grandchild's growing up.

I was brought up in the era of "children should be seen but not heard." Even so, I cherish the freedom allowed me to sit quietly and listen to the after dinner grown-up conversation. I learned much that way and when I lost interest, a "may I be excused?" always released me for other pursuits.

One of the wisest grandmothers I know suggests that your home should have a special character for the grandkids. She favours an atmosphere of peace and fun. It is your privilege to establish your own brand of atmosphere – one which attracts and nurtures your grandchildren. In a time of latch-key kids, split homes, one-parent families, you may be the one to provide that steadfast core of love and fun and peace and warmth.

While visiting a dear friend, I noted a beautifully worked needle-point sampler on the wall which read:

There's no place like home
Except grandma's.

On learning that it had been the gift of her daughter-in-law, I realized that my friend had succeeded in creating the right ambiance in her home for her grandchildren. That this quality had been recognized by her daughter-in-law was high praise indeed.

Special Places

Should you be fortunate enough to live out in the country or possess a summer cottage, you will be an instant hit with your grandchildren. Most nuclear families live in towns or cities and the parents maintain a structured after-school life for their progeny, consisting of swimming lessons, Scout or Brownie meetings, ballet classes or baseball practices.

Let these small over-organized beings loose in the country and soon they will be answering quite happily your query "Where did you go?" with "Out!" and "What did you do?" with "Nothing!"

I happen to have a cottage where feet on sofas and wet bathing-suited bottoms on chairs pose no problems. "Don'ts" go pretty well out the window with the only rules being those which have to do with the safety of the children and the sanity of the adults. Chores are few and are quickly disposed of when friends come banging on the screen door. My cottage possesses no TV and, once the kids have gotten over their withdrawal symptoms, they settle readily into a variety of creative activities.

In the hope that you might draw up a similar list, I am going to share some of my most cherished memories of those visits to my cottage by my grandchildren:

- Early morning walks when we just listen to birdsongs
- Watching a thunderstorm rage down on the lake
- Sitting on the front steps looking at the stars and singing all the 'star' songs we know
- Enjoying concerts planned in every detail by the children
- Ballet dancing on the front lawn
- Quiet chats and intimate confidences on the old white swing
- Competitive croquet games and races around the house
- Watching a toddler discover, with amazement, the sunbeam on his hand
- Listening to my son explain 'wind' to his 2-year old daughter

- Being soundly trounced at board games, from Candyland to Scrabble

- Satiating healthy appetites and not always with parent-approved foods

Though I stated that being soundly trounced at a game was a cherished memory, my granddaughter who kept the score, sees me as most unhappy. The bilingual comments reflect the fact that she is in a French immersion program at school, and that, like most of us, she loves to win.

As I write this, a collage emerges of swimming, suntanned bodies, wild flowers, tennis, trees, music, charades, books, laughter, loving looks, teddy bears, grubby hands, shells, toy boats, rocks, dominoes, quarrels, marshmallow roasts, and I long again for the arrival of summer.

Special Occasions

Should you be a grandmother who adores the hustle and bustle of festive occasions, ignore this section completely. But the comment of one, who stated that she preferred not to visit at Christmas because it was such a "grabby" time as far as the grandchildren were concerned, led me to write it.

An honest assessment of the various aspects of such visits and a grandmother's participation in them surely deserves some attention.

Christmas

In our family we celebrate Christmas so that's what I'm going to discuss. However, I am sure that no matter what major holiday you celebrate, you will find this helpful.

I readily admit that most grandmothers, especially the many widows amongst us, crave companionship at this time. But we must recognize that we are not the central attraction. Santa Claus has taken over.

Pre-Christmas Atmosphere

If I arrive a few days before Christmas, I like to defuse somewhat the over-stimulation of the pre-Christmas atmosphere. I bring small extra presents to be opened before Christmas. These are usually books which we can share.

Attending carol-singing concerts or church pageants with the whole family gives you a chance to stress the religious aspects of the holiday. Or be the one to set up that crèche which your own children enjoyed years ago.

Helping the grandchildren make or shop for presents for their parents is another way of giving their mother a chance to catch up on those last minute chores.

Finally, reading Christmas favourites and entering so gratefully into the warm glow of the family's decorating of the tree or hanging up the stockings is a quiet pleasure to be cherished before Santa deposits the gifts under the tree.

Gifts

A great many grandmothers who grew up during the depression years expressed concern at the quantity and expense of the presents showered on their grandchildren. One wrote plaintively, "Christmas and Birthday presents become a chore, as the children get older, especially if they live far away and you don't know their needs. Sometimes it is hard to adjust to the 'has everything' generation."

Some, with modest means, felt unable to compete. Grandma's hand-knit sweater soon lay swamped by the "hot" toy of the day. As one child put it, "I don't like soft presents." A knitting-efficient grandmother soon got the message.

But all is not lost. Sit back and enjoy the magic of a child's smile when, having ripped off that expensive wrapping paper, he comes upon the very thing asked for from Santa. Remember, your toque and cosy mittens, your carefully chosen games or book will come into its own when the "tumult and the shouting dies."

Have the thrill of watching a granddaughter proudly model that perfect Christmas dress which you made for her. Above all, do not be dismayed or irritated as your grandchildren sit amid the debris from several dozen carefully selected gifts and ask, "Are there any more for me?"

Allen Carter, chief child psychologist at the Institute of Living in Hartford, states that if the kids in question aren't beyond the pre-school stage, you shouldn't expect anything but that. "When they're still young, by nature they're self-centred. It's normal for them to want everything they can get" Carter says. He adds, "By the time children are five or six, they should understand that giving is part of the holidays too and the self-centredness should be less extreme. By the time the children are seven or eight, they should have learned to modulate their acquisitive desires. If they haven't, it's a problem," Carter says, and goes on to point out,

> "Not that parents should expect grown-up propriety from kids. The hope of getting more is a perfectly normal reaction in light of what adults have made of the holiday. There's tremendous anticipation (about Christmas morning) over stimulating for most kids. When they reach the end of unwrapping the presents, there's a kind of natural let-down at that point. The anticipation had been extreme. It's not possible to come down really gently. Every child experiences some of that every Christmas."

Pediatric psychologist Karen Anderssen adds, "The true spirit of the holidays is not something we were born with. Children rely on adults to teach them what sharing and caring are about."

"And if you are faced with 'Are there any more for me' questions, engage the children in play with toys they did get," Anderssen says, but adds, "if children are surrounded by new things but are whining for more, it could be they are looking for something else. That something else is likely to be time and attention."

Who is better able to supply just these elements than a watchful and understanding grandma?

You can be an example to your grandchildren in the gracious receiving of gifts. Those created by the children themselves, such as egg cartons gaily decorated to hold your earrings or plastic tubs emblazoned with painted hearts are more precious to any good granny than the most expensive gift chosen unbeknownst to the child giving it. But, whatever it is, love it, wear it, cherish it and express heartfelt thanks for it.

While on the subject of thanking, I found that some grandmothers described the hurt they felt when the presents they shopped for so carefully, or toiled over so painstakingly were not even acknowledged.

I have always considered a thank-you given to me verbally on the spot or over the phone would let any of my grandchildren off the hook as far as a thank-you was concerned. You may not agree. One irate grandfather wrote to "Dear Abby" telling of a grown-up grandchild to whom he sent cheques regularly and from whom he never received a word of thanks. Her advice was to send the next cheque unsigned. That would guarantee action!

Seeing a child wearing something you have given them or having them tell you of the fun they had with the toy you chose for them is surely the ultimate thanks. Lest you think that I don't enjoy receiving thank-you notes from my grandchildren, let me assure you that is not so. I keep every one they send and then write a letter in reply telling them how glad I am to hear from them.

Thanksgiving Dinner

"Over the river and through the woods
To Grandmother's house we go!"

This joyous song of old may bring delight or horror into the soul of the welcoming grandmother. Usually sundry relatives arrive to share this meal. Putting aside the stereotypical uncle who over imbibes or the crotchety old dear who bores, this can be a wonderful occasion for the grandchildren to enjoy an extended family.

Grandma can often be the catalyst to jog memories of the past and, in this sharing, long-gone family members live again. The conviviality of the meal should not be jarred by insistence upon Johnny's eating his entire broccoli or Jenny's taking at least two spoonfuls of that glamourous chestnut-oyster dressing. Would you consider it heresy to suggest that the young and restless should be excused from the table while it is being cleared for dessert and even that they should help with this chore? Encourage their involvement in this festive occasion just as you accept gratefully their parent's offers to bring along favourite dishes and/or help with the cleaning up.

After all have gone home and at last you have your feet up, ask yourself if the staging of such an event has been a joyous one. If it has, you have received ample reward for your efforts. If on the other hand, the whole affair has become a nightmare of planning, shopping and cooking which has left you emotionally and physically exhausted, have the courage to say so.

Today's emphasis on frank communication will not be a surprise to your nearest and dearest. They may have just needed that honest statement from you to give them the opportunity of establishing their own tradition in their own homes, with you as a honoured guest.

One grandparent always assured his children and grandchildren that their visit gave him a double pleasure. He loved to see them come and he loved to see them go! The same sentiment is expressed more subtly in Gladys Hasty Carroll's novel, "Unless You Die Young." A family reunion is drawing to a close – "I'm so lucky", thinks Grandmother Alice, "I'm probably the luckiest woman in the world, they all came. Every single one of them came. We've had a lovely day. And *now* they're getting ready to go home."

What a Grandmother Is

This "essay" was written by an 8-year old youngster in Grade 3, published in The Langley Advance and read on the CBC Radio.

A grandmother is a lady who has no children of her own so she likes other people's little girls. A grandfather is a man grandmother. He goes for walks with the boys and they talk about fishing and tractors and things like that.

Grandmas don't have to do anything except be there. They are old so they shouldn't play hard or run. It's enough if they drive us to the supermarket where the pretend horse is, and have lots of dimes ready. Or if they take us for a walk they should slow down past things like pretty leaves or caterpillars. They should never say hurry up. Usually they are fat but not too fat to tie kids' shoes. They wear glasses and funny underwear and they take their teeth and gums off.

It's better if they don't typewrite or play cards except with us. They don't have to be smart only answer questions like why dogs hate cats or how come God isn't married.

They don't talk baby talk like visitors do because it is hard to understand. When they read to us they don't skip or mind if it is the same story again. Everyone should try to have one, especially if you don't have TV because grandmas are the only grownups who have got time.

Chapter 4

The Fine Art of Spoiling

"She spoils me good."
– Grandchild

"Spoiling is our prerogative."
– Grandmother

IN MY BRAINSTORMING SESSIONS with children from Grades 1-6, I always asked if they felt that their grandmothers spoiled them. If you could have seen the gleeful sparkle in their eyes as they assured me that it was one of the things that grandmothers did best, you might think again about spoiling. Actually only fifty percent of the grandmas surveyed admitted that they *did* spoil and just a paltry thirty percent believed that a grandmother *should* spoil.

"To spoil" as defined in the dictionary is: to impair or damage or harm the character of someone by unwise treatment or excessive overindulgence.

To a grandchild spoiling is something quite different. One sees it as granny bringing treats and presents and taking her to interesting places. Another sees it as grandma listening to him and taking his side. Yet another perceptive child gave this sensitive response, "She's the one who thinks you're wonderful."

To me that last response puts spoiling in its proper perspective. Spoiling to a grandparent is the giving of *unconditional love.*

Surely no loving grandmother wishes to impair, damage or harm and no wise one wishes to overindulge.

How can we unconditionally love our grandchildren? Let us count the ways:

By Giving Them Quality Time

Once you are a grandmother you often have time in abundant supply. Turn it into quality time with those ready-to-be-spoiled grandchildren. Listen to them as individuals. Be understanding of their problems. Someone once told me there are no problem children, just children with problems. Cultivate that "third ear" which can discern that a grandson who says he hates his older brother is probably really saying that he hates being a sibling.

Praise them. An educational consultant, Richard P. Gallagher, suggests that this is a specific thing you can do to reinforce in positive ways a child's self-image.

"Praise by words and by a hug, a smile, a hand on the shoulder, anything that suggests warmth, approval, understanding… Praise everything. This includes the child's friendliness, kindness, generosity, enjoyment of learning, good sportsmanship, anything at all."

I concluded that I must have succeeded in this aspect when a card came to me from my granddaughter on which she wrote enthusiastically, if not humbly, "To a wonderful Grandmother from a wonderful Granddaughter!"

The grandmother who made tapes of favourite bedtime stories for her far away grandchildren knew the power of her loving voice as a cementing force in their relationship.

Share television programs with them. One of the most enjoyable experiences I had recently was watching "Anne of Green

Gables" with an 8-year old granddaughter. To see her acceptance of such sterling values as imagination, honesty, concern for others and respect for education was heartwarming.

My conversation with two older granddaughters after we had viewed a frank episode on "De Grassi Junior High" was a revelation. I was amazed by their emotional maturity and by their understanding of the temptations involved in certain relationships. Honesty compels me to admit, too, that I was saddened to see the innocence of childhood being challenged so soon.

Charles Dickens must have felt the same when in "Hard Times" he describes a teacher who is poised before a class of small children, "He seemed a kind of cannon loaded to the muzzle with facts and prepared to blow them clean out of the region of childhood at one discharge." I would be content to find the balance for my grandchildren among too much childhood, too little childhood, and none at all, wouldn't you? Dickens also said of children that we should be "ever careful that they should have a childhood of the mind no less than of the body."

Write letters or cards letting them know you are thinking of them. Take them to places different from the usual family outings. Be the one to introduce them to a museum or art galley, a ballet or theatrical production or a fine restaurant.

Make occasions for doings things separately with each grandchild. In larger families a child rarely gets this one-on-one attention. Frank McKenna, the former premier of the province of New Brunswick, tells about the influence of his grandmother. "My grandmother, Mary McKenna, gave me my desire to learn, to read, and to strive for excellence. She gave me her undivided attention, to the point where I was more like a first child."

By Giving Them Things

More affluent grandmothers enjoy the freedom of indulging their grandchildren in material ways. They like to be the one to buy the expensive toy or piece of sporting equipment. Others get a thrill shopping for their grandchildren and finding just the right thing for that certain child.

Grandchildren often commented on the generosity of their grandmas. They certainly seemed to equate a grandmother's visit with treats and presents. This is a valid expectation surely; for what self-respecting granny would come empty-handed to visit her grandkids? The chocolate chip cookies or the small toy may be classed as an indulgence, but as a character-damaging overindulgence – what errant nonsense!

By Giving Them Outward Expressions of Love

Time and again I was told by young children in the early grades that grandmas were loveable, that they like to hug and kiss. Never was this admitted in a derisive war; rather it was given as one more pleasing grandmotherly quality.

Some older youngsters had a few negative comments to make "She's mean and crabby... She's fussy about your manners, how you dress... She's weird but nice." Generally, though, they saw their grandmothers as loving, kind, considerate, thoughtful and even terrific, spectacular and fantastic. However, no mention was made by these older ones of overt signs of affection.

Grandmothers, on the other hand, wrote frequently of the delight of snuggles and cuddles. Do I speak for other widows when I confess that warm hugs and kisses from grandchildren fill a very deep need for some loving arms about one?

Enough has been written about the nurturing quality of touching and holding to qualify this aspect of spoiling as one which must be encouraged. Children grow and blossom in an atmosphere of love. If you can bring love and tenderness into the life of an unloved or unappreciated grandchild, you will contribute immeasurably to that child's healthy growth.

Leo Buscaglia, certainly the huggiest man in the world, readily admitted to an audience that his way of expressing love might not be for everyone. You may have a grandchild who does not care to climb onto your lap for kisses and hugs. Do not feel it as rejection if instead he squirms out of your embrace or she refuses to be kissed. These are often the very active or curious children who must be on the move, playing with that favourite toy or discovering how something works. Join them in their play or assist them in their discovery and the warm look you receive or the sincere request for your participation will be the way that child chooses to express love. Be content with it.

Pet names and endearments are all part of spoiling too. I have young grandsons whom I call "Lamb-chop" and "Love-pot" and *so far*, they haven't objected. My heart melts when my grandkids end their telephone conversation with me with the ritual chant, 'Kiss, kiss, hug, hug. Love you!' It is my belief that children who can express their emotions readily by word or deed will have an easier time in future relationships.

By Giving Them Support

I value that time honoured maxim that children should be given both roots and wings. As their connection with an older generation, you do help to give them roots. But do you have the courage to give them wings? Do you encourage your granddaughter to tackle jobs and experiences that you have been brought up to believe were solely in the male domain? Do you support your grandson when he takes off in a direction different from that expected by his parents or family tradition? What if he wants to be a plumber instead of an engineer, an artist instead of a banker, a farmer instead of a doctor? Are you on his side or do you help his family, by your silence, to clip his wings?

As a new grandmother, you will not be confronted by questions of such magnitude for some time. If or when you are, remember that many children saw grandma taking their side as one of her most endearing qualities. Don't let them down. While having my hair done recently, I asked the personable young hairdresser if he had a good relationship with his grandmother. He replied, "I certainly do. We often go partying together and whenever I need help or comfort I head for grandma's. She's never critical." So you see this kind of spoiling has no time limit.

This chapter opened with the ungrammatical statement "She spoils me good." Voiced enthusiastically by a Grade 3 pupil. The dictionary would find it a contradiction in terms but it reinforces my opinion that spoiling is a grandmother's function and that its outcome is indeed good.

"The schoolchildren assured me that spoiling was one of the things that grandmothers did best."

Some testimonials to that effect:

My gran cooks for me. She cooks brownies, cakes, muffins, cookies and pies. I love my grandmother.
– Grade 3 pupil

My grandpa and grandma love me a lot. My grandpa taught me how to play rummy and crazy eights. My grandma takes me out a lot to dinner and gives me dessert.
– Grade 4 pupil

She always shops with me. I never come out of the mall without something. She gets me so many presents.
– Grade 3 pupil

My Mom's mom spoils me a lot. But sometimes she is really mean. Other than that my grandma is great.
– Grade 5 pupil

Grandmothers have to be kind and generous to their grandchildren. – Grade 6 pupil

My granny is sweet and kind. She spoils me a lot because I am her only granddaughter.
– Grade 6 pupil

Grandmothers are very nice. My grandma always bakes cakes when she invites me over for supper.
– Grade 5 pupil

My grandmother spoils me. She takes me every weekend from Friday till late Sunday night.
– Grade 5 pupil

No wonder we love our grandchildren.
One was spotted picking petals off a daisy and
singing softly,

Loves me, Loves me lots
Loves me, Loves me lots!

~

Some Grandmas have limousines
And the biggest homes you've ever seen
But my Grandma's the best by far
For she has got a cookie jar.

Chapter 5

Pass It On

LIVING WITH "IF ONLY" is difficult, frustrating and above all, sad. For instance, if only I had asked my mother and father more about their relatives, if only I had made a tape of Aunt Martha's stories of her fascinating travels, if only I had taken the time to convey my love of art (music, literature, nature) to my children.... The list is endless but in it are clues to what you may deem important to pass onto your grandchildren.

No two grandmothers look alike. Their interests vary and their tolerance of noise or mess is by no means the same. Nevertheless, they are alike in that they do have some special things to pass to their grandchildren. This may be the time to interject that the two grandmothers in an average family should not be in competition. One of my granddaughters acknowledged this when she told her maternal grandmother, a skilled potter, "You know, Granny, you show me how to do things and my other Granny explains things." In other words, we complement each other. What a compliment that was!

Family History and Traditions

You, my little apple,
Sprang from a sturdy tree.
Branches of generations
Embrace you tenderly.

Judith Levy

You are now approaching the age when you may well be the sole repository of your family history. Treasured stories of parents or relatives should be passed on to small receptive ears. Enter the electronic age and consider recording these cherished memories.

Is it beyond your capabilities to create a family tree for your grandchildren? Accompany it with as many pictures of those on it as is possible. I was given Judith Levy's beautiful book, "Grandmother Remembers," which, when I complete it, will be a written heirloom for my grandchild.

A grandmother writes that in her desire to give her grandchildren a sense of family and of their heritage as Scottish Canadians, she teaches them stories, games and crafts learned from her own granny.

Though children like listening to stories of your childhood, they also enjoy hearing of the antics of their parents – the naughtier the better. But they simply adore anecdotes about themselves. As one grandma put it, "The pleasant things you remember from their 'tiny' days can be repeated year after year and maybe even gain in the telling. They help increase a child's sense of identity and worth."

Arts and Crafts

Those of you with artistic and domestic talents owe it to your grandchildren to share your skills. You could be the one to introduce a small child to the delight and mess of finger painting or play dough. Baking and decorating cookies for special occasions is an activity appreciated by all your grandchildren – irrespective of gender. Rolling out pie crust until it is grey is no hindrance to the final taste of a little one's very own jam tart. Older children may have mothers who are too busy to teach them to knit, sew, embroider, sketch or model. You can be the one to guide their hands in the pursuit of what may become a life-long hobby for them.

My Grandmother is very loving.
I love her very much.
She likes Nature. So do I.
– Grade 5 pupil

LADY BUG

SPIDER

Grasshopper

FLY

Nature

Recipe for Preserving Children

1 grass grown field
1/2 dozen children or more
1 brook
Pebbles
Several dogs (puppies if in season)

Into the field, pour children and dogs, allowing to mix well. Pour brook over pebbles till slightly frothy and the right temperature for wading. When children are nicely brown, cool in warm tub. When dry, serve with milk and freshly baked bread.

Many grandmothers are ardent gardeners or avid birdwatchers or dedicated nature lovers. Encourage any child to kneel beside you and dig in the garden, teaching them which plants are the flowers and which are the weeds. Give them the joy of planting seeds or bulbs and watching them grow. Nature walks, bird sighting expeditions, fishing trips and viewing sunsets could open up, especially for a city child, a world of wonders. Reinforce their burgeoning interests in this world by giving them a subscription to any of the many splendid children's nature magazines – a birthday gift they can enjoy twelve times a year.

Sports

A grandmother relates: I had two grandsons for a couple of weekends. To keep them happy I took them walking and running. Later, after they were home, the 6-year old referred to me as 'old.' His mother said this was not so. From another corner of the room came a slight laugh and then the 4-year old asked his mother, "Did you ever see her run?"

Various grandchildren I interviewed assured me they had grandmothers who would play ball with them, or would take them sliding, skating, skiing, swimming, hiking and exploring. Though I tried not to show it, I was somewhat incredulous on learning of a grandmother who roller-skated, another who played football and of one stalwart soul who rode a motorcycle!

Keeping fit, eating well and thinking positively are the touchstones for healthy living. You will need to practice all three if you want to keep up with your active grandchildren.

For those grandmothers whose constitutions are not too robust, your role as an enthusiastic spectator at a grandchild's soccer game, swim meet or ballet recital will be much appreciated by that striving child.

Adopting a healthier lifestyle, for the sake of those concerned children who told me they worried about losing their grandparents, might be something you should consider. One little girl told the older of her two grandmothers, "You are the most precious because you might 'conk' soon."

One of my granddaughters was found crying inconsolably one night because it had occurred to her that her grannies weren't going to be around forever. She was finally comforted when I assured her firmly that I was doing everything I could think of to ensure that I would be around to dance at her wedding. Dry-eyed, she asked bluntly, "Who with?" Whether she was referring to her future husband or my dancing partner is a matter of speculation.

Manners

The lyrics of an old song, "You always hurt the one you love, the one you shouldn't hurt at all," come to mind when I witness the terrible verbal abuse to which small children are too often subjected. I wince at scenes I have watched at supermarkets and wonder what the fallout of such scenes could be on the future behaviour of these children as parents.

As a caring grandmother how can we help our grandchildren to react well with other people?

Firstly, recall that good manners have been called the oil which lubricates the wheels of social interaction. Obviously, there is no better way of teaching good manners than by being mannerly yourself.

Secondly, analyze your reasons for expecting your grandchildren to be polite. Ask yourself if you see them as loved and valued friends or as small people who must be kept in their place and be a credit to you in public.

Grandchildren registered disapproval of a grandmother "who was fussy about manners", "who expected you to dress old-fashioned with a dress and even a slip" or "who makes you eat like a gentleman." These comments would seem to indicate that a grandmother who nags about manners is resented and possibly rightly so. Is it polite to criticize loudly a child's manners at a family dinner or in a restaurant? Would you do that to a beloved friend?

I read an article recently which was entitled, "Good Manners Make Good Children." It was excerpted from Judith Martin's book "Miss Manners' Guide to Perfect Children." I have always felt that her pronouncements were written in an entertaining if somewhat tongue-in-cheek way. Be that as it may, she states that children are born unruly and must be trained to behave. She, as you may guess, believes in manners for children. She abhors the idea, fashionable for the last two decades that the child is born good, creative and wise, and that education should therefore consist of drawing out from the child what is there – feelings and even opinions – rather than putting things in, such as the accumulated experience and wisdom of society.

As a wise and experienced grandmother should you consider putting things in, as she suggests? Whatever your reaction may be to her advice, perhaps you will at least agree with me that "Please", "Thank you" and "Excuse Me" are not yet outmoded. Your use of these "magic words" yourself and your gentle insistence that your grandchildren use them in your presence can be the first bold step in this daunting challenge of passing on good manners. For daunting it is.

I recall vividly my son's astoundingly good manners when we dined out with friends one evening. I was absolutely flabbergasted as I watched him exhibit all the niceties of polite behaviour which I had tried desperately to instill in him. On the way home I praised him to the skies. His chief reaction was, "Being polite is terribly tiring." The next day he was back to normal; but I took satisfaction in the fact that he at least knew what to do when the occasion arose.

Cultural Pursuits

Imagination

The bird Imagination
That flies so far, that dies so soon
Her wings are coloured like the sun,
Her breast is coloured like the moon.
Weave her a chain of silver twist,
And a little hood of scarlet wool,
And let her perch upon your wrist
And tell her she is beautiful.

Elinor Wylie

In an attempt to show young children how to look at works of art, I visit elementary schools a couple of mornings a week. Armed with a portfolio of art reproductions and my undying enjoyment of teaching, I do my best to keep their attention. I usually start with a panegyric about imagination. When I asserted that it was one of our most precious possessions, I asked a Grade 3 student what "precious" meant. "Fragile," said he. What a wonderful word to describe that need to handle carefully this right-brain quality! You would think he had read Elinor Wylie's beautiful poem.

"Imagination is more important than knowledge for knowledge is limited, while imagination embraces the entire world" Albert Einstein

Barbara Florio Graham writes: "We're a dedicated left-brain, right-handed society that rewards logical, linear, orderly thinking. Creative people wander outside the parameters, daydream, doodle and ask irrelevant questions." She adds that recent research indicates that high activity in the right side of the brain contributes to optimism and overall happiness.

Another article on creativity headed by that quotation of Albert Einstein's said that the primary secret to creativity was to let your imagination run wild. I now felt justified in asking my pupils to exercise their imagination as they viewed the reproductions. Later I reflected that grandmothers could well be the ones to spark this right-brain activity.

A Grandchild's Plea

I am a little child
I paint fearlessly
I build recklessly
I write originally
I sing rapturously

I hammer loudly
Never quell my creativity
Just refine it.

If you are now convinced of the value of nurturing imagination, here are a few ways in which to do so.

Literature, music, art, dance, drama, scientific discovery – all products of fertile imaginations – are readily available in our libraries, art galleries, concert halls and museums.

Be the one to open the door to such treasures for a young grandchild. Do prior research before taking a child to, say, an art gallery. Decide which paintings you think would interest her. Keep the visit short and sweet. Lunch and a visit to a gallery bookstore to select a postcard of a favourite work of art could complete a memorable experience for both you and your grandchild.

The age and thus the attention span of a child should be considered before embarking on any of these pursuits. How many of you have seen young children at evening performances of long ballets snoozing through most of the performance? Surely a matinee would have been a better choice.

Don't let your love of a certain play, opera, ballet or symphony blinds you to the fact that it may be far beyond the understanding or enjoyment of a young child. Children's theatre, tours for youngsters through museums and sing-along concerts by such artists as Raffi are all fine ways to introduce another dimension into the lives of your TV fettered grandchildren.

Simpler and less expensive ways of stimulating a child's imagination are right at hand for any granny with a fine-working imagination of her own.

Encourage the littlest ones to play imaginatively. I despise battery-operated toys which demand nothing of the small child except they watch it move or listen to it talk. Sit down on the floor with the 3-year old and his Fisher Price "little people" and have a ball making up places for them to go and things for them to do. Soon the grandchild is naming each one and organizing an adventure for them. My 2-year old grandson left one of his people at my cottage. When I returned it to him the following Easter, he exclaimed, "Look, its Annie!"

Puppet shows, charades, and plays they make up themselves are all good activities for the older grandchildren. Participate in them or at least be an enthusiastic and receptive audience. Playing school, store, or building a harbour at the beach or a tent under a blanket-covered table may seem old hat to you but for these new youngsters they are a journey into the world of imagination. Take their hands and lead them on the way.

Enough cannot be said about inculcating a love of reading and story-telling as a means of bringing about creative thinking. Professor Jody Potts teaches several steps that she says will set free anyone's creativity: "First you have to feed the mind. Creativity is treating your mind as a kaleidoscope. You want to let in as many crystals as you can and then turn them so they form new patterns." What better way to feed those young minds than reading to them?

There are excellent children's books on the market. You might make a habit of reading the reviews of them and selecting the perfect one for that special grandchild.

Reading stories or poems aloud is well within the capabilities of any grandma. This enhances the children's listening skills and makes them aware of the beauty of the spoken word.

Do not neglect "the ageless power of Mother Goose" begs Joan Bodger in her illumination article with that title. She also points out that Mother Goose is made up "of quirky people, brilliant images, carefully distilled plots and some of the most beautiful lines in the English language":

I saw a peacock with a fiery tail
I saw a blazing comet…
A silver nutmeg and a golden pear…
One misty, moisty morning…
Over the hills and far way…

Should your copy of Mother Goose be lost you might treat yourself to Iona and Peter Opies' *Oxford Nursery Rhyme Book*. When it appeared in 1955, Clifton Fadiman wrote in his review: "If your child does not like this book, don't get rid of the book, get rid of the child." Since it is very expensive, it is suggested that you go to a library, read the introduction and browse through the rhymes.

Making up bedtime stories has always been one of my favourite ways of entertaining my grandchildren. In these stories one grandchild plays the stellar role, does magical things and had fantastic adventures. Early on they were labelled "Think" stories by a grandchild – since they did not come out of a book, I suppose. Recently I spun one of these tales for Peter (Age 3). He was fascinated with my first story of his exploits. The next night I tried to change the plot but he wanted a repetition of the previous night's story. On the third night he insisted on telling me the story himself. I gave in reluctantly because I love devising bizarre and complicated sequels. I realized then, that listening to a child's flights of imagination was equally important.

With the wealth of beautifully-written children's books, you might hesitate to create your own stories or verses. The final paragraph of Joan Bodger's splendid article addresses just that quandary:

"Does this mean that we should give up telling family stories or making up nonsense rhymes for our children? Of course not. They are like love letters. Few can survive being published to the light of day, but their power to touch the individual heart cannot be gainsaid. Two Eyes' table on the hill was spread with many dishes. If we are going to share the feast, let there be literary tales and folktales, rhymes and songs and poetry and how our family came to Canada stories and how mother met daddy stories. And how I used to spit up my orange juice. Everyone loves a story. Everyone has a story."

Values

> "I am concerned about how one's own child is coping
> with being a parent and wonder to what extent the
> values I instilled in him still prevail." *A Grandmother*

Most of us came from a generation in which regular attendance at a religious institution was the norm. We look about us today and see many of our grandchildren being brought up in a completely secular way.

Little ones will love the Bible stories and songs on which you were nurtured. Sharing, helping others, resisting evil are learned values; they do not come to a child naturally. Some acquaintance with the religious wisdom of the past can give your grandchild a glimpse of another dimension of living in an increasingly materialistic world.

I recall a summer I spent as a counsellor in a camp for underprivileged children. One Sunday I sat in church beside the toughest, roughest small boy in the whole camp. When the minister announced the next hymn, this urchin shouted an ecstatic "Dare to be a Daniel. Hot dog!" Face shining; he joined in heartily in singing that hymn with rollicking chorus:

> Dare to be a Daniel,
> Dare to stand alone.
> Dare to have a purpose firm,
> And dare to make it known.

I've often wondered how that boy turned out and why the memory of his freckled face raised in song has remained with me over the years.

Spiritual wellness has been defined as a caring centre within each of us that promotes sharing, love, and compassion for others. By exhibiting these qualities ourselves we may make the greatest impact on our grandchildren. Praising them for their acts of sharing, tolerance or compassion will reinforce these worthwhile attributes.

Proud grandmas recount:

♡ Even at four years of age my middle grandchild was very caring and sweet-natured. One of his Jewish friends was upset one day and had to go to the bathroom. My grandson accompanied him and returned with his arm around his friend asking, "But why are you cut off?"

♡ My twelve year old grandson has just informed me that he plans to become a medical doctor when he grows up so that he will be able to take care of me and his grandpa for free.

♡ We have always said, "I love you" to our kids as we tucked them into bed. While tucking my grandson (age 3) into bed one night, I said, "I love you," as usual, as he looked up at me. You could see he was struggling for something to say in reply. Finally, it came out. "Your face looks very nice in your clothes."

♡ My daughter was hospitalized recently and shared a room with an elderly woman, who should have been elsewhere, but there was no place for her to go, and no one came near her. My grandsons were curious, so I explained the old lady's tragic situation. The grandson who had just turned seven, said, "We'd never let that happen to you Granny, because you are the one who gave us our mommy."

A Grandmother's Prayer

Let me give my grandchild gifts,
Not just toys, but other things
Like treasured dreams and memories
That give a child both roots and wings.

Let me help with little things,
To teach someone to tie a shoe,
To answer funny questions now
And always know just what to do.

Let me show that what is old
A child may find completely new,
And know what once delighted me
Makes my grandchild happy too.

Let me use this special time,
Feeling blessed by circumstance
For sometimes being a Grandma is
A mother's happy Second Chance.

Jill Wolf

Chapter 6
A Second Chance

"I think I have more time to appreciate or maybe I'm wiser than when our children were young. It seems such a blessing to have a second chance." J.W., a grandmother

It was astounding how many grandmothers stated that being a grandmother was a second chance:

- ♡ At being slightly silly and playful
- ♡ At enjoying wee babies
- ♡ At having a child take your hand in trust
- ♡ At watching the progress and development of young minds
- ♡ At hugging small bodies
- ♡ At having more people to love and be loved

Time

Actually all they were saying was that they were being given one more chance to do quality parenting. But time is the essential factor. We can all remember those years when our children were small and often it seems in retrospect a blur of getting meals, making beds, doing laundry, finding lost mittens, admonishing erring progeny, etc.

Did we have time then to reflect that these were the most fulfilling and productive days we might ever enjoy? I suspect not. But now we do have the time to take on the fascinating challenge of another go at parenting.

Change

First you must recognize that your grandchildren are growing up in a different world. They are facing more distractions, more temptations and greater expectations. You must ask yourself if you are prepared to change your mind about some rather old-fashioned ideas which your family believed to be true.

If you want to see a grandchild's eyes glaze over with boredom, start your conversation or should I say, sermon with "When I was your age we didn't do this, that, or the next thing."

Grandparenting is your passport to the future. Don't hang back in the past, lamenting the things you must leave behind.

Judith Viorst in her excellent book, *Necessary Losses*, writes that grandparenting frees grandma and grandpa to be "more loving, more tender, patient, generous, you name it, than they had ever been as mother and father. No longer concerned with instilling moral values, no longer in charge of discipline and rules, no longer dedicated to building character, they become their best selves." This very thought was expressed time and again by the grandmothers interviewed.

Understanding

As one grows older there is a powerful need to share the experiences, the wisdom and the philosophy acquired as life went by.

This is the role of mentor and happy is she who has an activity which gives her the opportunity to play the part. I truly believe that grandmothering is one such activity.

To be a mentor to your grandchild, you must be prepared to listen and observe first, and advise later. I wrote before about that "third ear" which hears behind the words and can alert an astute grandmother to, for instance, a difficult child's inner needs.

Giving advice is useless if based solely on out-dated ideas or maxims. Today a grandmother has ample resources at her finger tips. Never were there more books, articles or programs on child-raising. Read, listen and learn. Then you can become a well-informed and understanding grandmother whom your grandchildren can trust with their problems and their confidences. You may even be able to offer their parents some advice – but don't count on it! Family counsellor Resa Eisen sees this aspect of grandmothering as a reciprocally revealing one.

Another thought-provoking article tells of a very successful American business woman who was born with the learning disability known as dyslexia. Kathy Kolbe believes being dyslexic gives her a different perspective on the world. With your grandchildren in mind, read what she has to say about testing and learning styles.

Kolbe said one of her goals is to persuade the business and educational communities that human beings don't all think the same way and that to measure their aptitude through rote-learning tests punishes those whose intellectual makeup keep them from mimicking their teachers or bosses.

"People should be risk takers, tenacious doers and problem solvers. Some of us like that we are called weird, but that's a compliment because it means we're willing to go beyond the norm and take chances."

"How do you teach a child to go beyond mimicking? Well, a good teacher should want his students to go beyond him, to improve on what he has done. And one way is to encourage mistakes. If we do everything right, then we're doing something wrong."

Another one of Kolbe's goals is to set the test world on its ear. She explained: "Tests don't accommodate two kinds of learning styles. By the third grade, our schools stop allowing children who exhibit these styles to excel."

Kolbe maintains that there are four distinct learning styles, or conations, which she defines as "natural tendencies in mental processes or behaviours directed toward action or change."

She identifies the two groups she thinks are rebuked by the educational community as "quick-starts" and "implementors." She calls the other two groups "fact-finders" and "follow-throughs."

Here's how she defines each group:

> **The Quick-Starts:** "They don't get good grades, but teachers may like them for their spirit and effort. They often become entrepreneurs because they don't want to go through a system to get where they're going. They don't like definitions. Say the word 'can't' to a quick-start and that's a guarantee he'll try it.
>
> *Quick-starts* don't like to read directions and don't want to hear the pros and cons on whether to start a project because they know the cons will outweigh the pros. They are innovators who will start something on a hunch. But if you tell a *quick-start* to research a plan and come up with a recommendation, you'll get a lousy report."

The Implementors: "They are three-dimensional and hands-on people, like surgeons, sculptors and craftsmen. They love to tinker, touch and feel. They have low interest in language and are not good communicators. They want to do things, but don't want to be told what to do.

I worry a lot about the *implementors* of the world. Language is a barrier to learning for them. They do not get good grades, and school is a terrible experience for them. They tend to be mostly male, they don't have a sense of colour, and they're often sentimental and involved in causes."

The Fact-Finders: "They get good grades in school and often become lawyers, corporate executives, researchers, and teachers. They are sensible, methodical and reliable. But if you tell a fact-finder to go out and implement an idea – he won't. He will not act until he's sure the idea will work.

If you tell a *fact-finder* he can't do something, he'll probably agree that he had better not try. *Fact-finders* are successful in the legal arena, where they can rely on precedent to support their actions."

The Follow-Throughs: "They are the office manager, grade school teachers and middle management people. They are punctual, orderly, dependable and diligent. They are usually the teacher's delight because they work hard and get good grades.

Follow-throughs are essential members of teams because they can be counted on to complete the task at hand. They are steady and true."

Kolbe identifies herself as both a *quick-start* and a *follow-through*. "I started my mail order business after some publishers in New York turned me down because they didn't think there was a market for the products. That's the *quick-start* side of me.

"But I wouldn't have stayed in business long if I hadn't been able to behave like a *follow-through* and everyday set aside time to go over mailing lists and inventory. And that's pretty frustrating for a dyslexic who's continually mistaking a typewriter for a word processor."

Communication

"I Never Promised You a Rose Garden" is that popular song which perfectly expresses the warning I should have offered as I wrote so encouragingly about this grandmother-grandchild relationship. Therefore in this penultimate chapter I must write of one of the thorniest problems to affect many grandmothers these days. This is the sad one of being denied access to their grandchildren because of a divorce, a separation or when a conflict arises between the parents and grandparents. This is a devastating experience for any grandparent, particularly when they see it as through no fault of their own.

There are various groups offering support to grandparents cut off from their grandchildren because of family conflicts.

Marilyn Lay, one of the founders of GRAND (Grandparents Requesting Access and Dignity) and herself a family counsellor states, "It's shocking, but children are made pawns in these conflicts and it's not surprising that it extends to grandparents. It's a reflection of how older people are looked upon by society. Their contribution to the growth and development of kids is not valued. Grandparents can play a beneficial role in a child's life. They offer unconditional doses of love, stability, continuity and often are the 'calm in the storm,' especially during family conflicts.

It goes without saying that whatever steps are taken must be taken by a tolerant, forgiving grandmother whose sole aim is to help her grandchildren assuage the trauma suffered when the grandchild and grandparent "connection" is disrupted.

I learned recently of a grandmother in California whose grandchild lives with a divorced parent in the East. She makes sure she sees the child at least twice a year and that they do memorable things together. Letters flow back and forth. The connection is strong because she makes it so. It is quite possible that in spite of your efforts, this link is broken. However, if distance or other circumstances separate you from your own grandchild, don't despair. There are children out there begging for a grandmother's love and attention.

A young parent from British Columbia wrote to me about the Volunteer Grandparents Society in her province in which she enrolled her two children with enriching benefits for the whole family.

In Ottawa there is another kind of grandparent volunteer program. Recognizing how her own children had gained from their grandparents, Cynthia LeDain, volunteer services coordinator for the school board, developed a program that brings the two generations together. (The seniors spend at least two hours a week with children in Grades 1 to 4, reading to them or just chatting.) She states that this program gives children a lifelong base for expressing themselves and communicating with others and fills a gap in the lives of many older people, giving them a chance to share their experience and love with a second generation.

June Callwood, a well known Canadian columnist, spoke of North York's Interlink Choir, consisting of seniors and young children, which were patterned on a similar choir seen on American TV. She made this astute observation, "The very old and the very new have been a good mix since the human race began. Young adults bear the stressful responsibility of family survival, so it usually falls to the tribe's tranquil elders to convey the cultural myths and ethos. Behavioural scientists believe that children derive steadiness from the grandparent's generation which can give them a past. Past is a bedrock; put your feet on it and you are calmly positioned to see for miles."

Acceptance

As the sub-title of this book *A Grandmother's First Handbook* suggests, this book is aimed at the new grandmothers of young children. But soon, all too soon, that child becomes a teenager and the generation gap between you widens dramatically. I found the answer to accepting this transitional phase in a fine article sent to me by a close friend and herself a splendid grandmother. It was written by Bob Greene in the Ottawa Sunday Herald. His last grandmother had just died, and, as he remembered her, he touched on one of the tough parts about being a grandparent. I quote from his column.

> "As you grow older as a grandparent, you must begin to accept the sad fact that most contacts with your grandchildren will be seen as an act of duty on their part. Perhaps an act of duty willingly carried out with love; but if you're a sharp grandparent, you will realize that every call and visit was probably preceded by a gentle suggestion that Grandma or Grandpa surely would appreciate a few words or a few minutes.
>
> That it seems, must be one of the hardest parts of being a grandparent; knowing that the world out there seems much more urgent and inviting to your grandchildren than a few hours spent with Grandma or Grandpa... and if you are the best kind of grand-

parent, you will not only accept that, but welcome it. You will know that it is good for your grandchildren to go out and greet their own lives fully... So you must cherish whatever hours you have, and take pride from afar that your grandchildren are on a daily basis creating their own universe – a universe that, if you are lucky, you will hear about.

I cannot think of a single time when my grandmother made me feel that I was deserting her by dashing off to be with my friends and now I can't help believing that she realized this was one of the most important roles a grandparent can play; to love without clasping, to love enough to let your grandchildren have their own lives."

It was Valentine's Day when I finished roughing out this chapter. I leafed through a collection of Valentine cards which had been sent to me by my grandchildren over the years. (Incidentally, should you ever need an ego-booster as a grandmother, browse through the Grandma's Birthday card section of the greeting card display and read through all the cards saying how wonderful you are.)

One Hallmark Valentine card expressed a sentiment any of us would like to hear voiced by an older or far-distant grandchild. Perhaps with a genuine attempt at taking a second chance at parenting, you just might hear it.

Grandmother, no matter how
grown up I may be
or how independent I feel
no matter the distance between us
or the time between visits

no matter what happens today
or tomorrow
there's one thing
you can always be sure of
How much I love you.

Happy Valentine's Day

Chapter 7

And Now It's Your Turn

IN MY INTRODUCTION I wrote that this book grew out of the wisdom and wonder of the many grandmothers who answered my questionnaire. It is only fitting that I share some of the insights in their answers to the following questions.

A) Do you differ as a grandmother from your own grandmother?

1. I think I've given more of myself to them than my mother gave to my children.

2. Grandparenting seems to be more fun for me. It is a more relaxed relationship.

3. My mother loved my children but she was more distant and critical.

4. She had more patience and understanding. She was a role model for Christian living.

5. I believe I am more affectionate and have more time and money to spend on them.

6. I don't play one child against another. I see them more as individuals, each supremely his or her own person.

7. She was partial to girls and I had three boys.

Summary: The majority of answers to this question affirmed that grandmothers of today perceived that they did differ from their own mothers. Sometimes sickness and distance were given as reasons for the poor contact between the generations. Criticism and stern discipline were also cited as a negative aspect of the way their mothers had acted as grandmothers.

However, from the sampling of answers given above, it is evident that the grandmothers of the past were both good and not so good. This probably holds true today, though many of the responses reveal that modern grandparents have more time to indulge in this role and have picked up sound psychological insights along the way. They see grandparenting as fun and find it a relaxed, loving relationship. One believed that today's grandchildren communicate more freely with their grandparents and, of course, saw this as a vast improvement.

B) Why are you more attached to some grandchildren than to others?

1. All twelve are wonderful and I love them all equally.

2. Those you have known well since birth and whose parents share them more tend to be favourites. You feel much closer to the grandchild you see most often.

3. It is not fair to compare a gentle 5-year old girl with a fractious 2-year boy, who will, I am sure, improve

with age. Some stages of development are more attractive than others.

4. A child in whom you can discern your own traits, personality or looks may make him or her more interesting to you.

5. I find myself giving more attention to and receiving more joy from the small ones.

6. I rarely see the grandchildren whose parents are divorced and therefore feel closer to the others.

7. One of my grandchildren is a Down's syndrome baby and is very special.

8. One personality can appeal more than another. I tend to prefer those who are loving and disciplined rather than demanding and self-centered.

Summary: Though over half of the grandmothers gave answers similar to the first given above, a goodly number provided other thought-provoking and extremely honest responses which I felt I must share with you. These acknowledged our own limitations as well as our realistic acceptance of facts.

C) What are some of the things that are not great about being a grandmother?

1. To be conscious of the need not to criticize or break the rules of behaviour or discipline which parents make.

2. Knowing that I'm growing older and will not be around when they have growing families of their own. When a grandchild observes that the Royal Doulton figurine of the wizened 'Balloon Lady' is you and the 'Top of the Hill' beauty is mommy.

3. Not being allowed to baby-sit. Being tired out after baby-sitting and the mess from having little ones around, which you aren't used to. Being asked to baby-sit too frequently.

4. Missing them when you live too far away. Wishing you could see more of them and be part of their lives.

5. More worries and concerns about grandchildren's development and values; about their health and happiness; about their parents' ability to cope with parenthood.

6. Seeing this complex world becoming more threatening to my grandchildren.

Summary: The majority answered this question at great lengths explaining that one of most difficult things about being a grandmother was the need to smother any hint of criticism about the raising of their grandchildren. Insight into this problem rightly has its place in a book dealing with the relationship between the grandmother and her adult children. All would admit that there is nothing as hurtful and disruptive as criticism, however well intended.

On the other hand it would be cowardly to watch in silence while a grandchild suffered either physical or verbal abuse. When the needs of the child are consistently ignored, it must surely be your duty as a caring grandmother to speak up.

A common criticism concerned the dreadful bedtime routines allowed by many new parents. Evenings which should have been a quiet time for adults to relax were made a horror, with parents allowing the over stimulated and exhausted child to be the centre of the adults' attention, including that of a disenchanted grandma. The magic of a routine of quiet play after supper, a warm bath and an enchanting bedtime story never seemed to occur to these parents; and, alas, grandma hesitated to suggest it lest she be accused of interfering.

A certain sadness pervades the frequent assertions that grandparents were not welcome as visitors or that they were used only as baby-sitters. One can but wonder how this breakdown in communications occurred and why it was allowed to persist. It should be understood by all that the best grandmothers are neither spongers nor doormats.

D) What do you gain as a person by being a grandmother?

1. Pride and self-esteem. A feeling of being wanted and needed.

2. The incredible delight of knowing that there is this extension of myself. An insight into life beyond my time – the grandchildren are my window on eternity.

3. The enjoyment of the love and respect of children.

4. Fulfillment – being a more complete person who is able to be involved with young people and their progress. Another chance to see human beings mature.

5. The bringing back of memories of my own children and my own childhood. A third childhood.

6. More common ground with my daughter. We can discuss the many difficulties of raising a child in this modern, women's lib, materialistic world. This tolerance has found its way into my attitudes and behaviour in other areas of life.

7. The joy of seeing my sons emerge as wonderful parents.

8. A whole new dimension of living. It has made me a much richer and more interesting person. It's a learning process and rounds out life as any experience would.

9. The happiness, pleasure and joy received from the grandchildren and their parents.

Summary: This question naturally evoked the most upbeat and positive answers. Whenever I felt doubts about writing this book, I re-read the many thoughtful answers and took heart. Yes, I reassured myself, I was right in asserting that the grandmother-grandchild relationship was a joyous and rewarding one. To you grandmothers who answered the questionnaire with such care and insight, I offer my profound thanks. This book could not have been written without your help.

E) How would you like to be remembered by your grandchildren?

1. As a kind, intelligent person whom they loved and will miss.

2. As someone they wanted to see and visit because I was happy, interesting and easy to talk to.

3. As a thoughtful, understanding person who loved all grandchildren as individuals.

4. As one who believed in a disciplined, responsible way of life, but tempered with love.

5. As a loving, caring person they could have fun with, talk to and count on when needed.

6. As one with faith in God, and hope for the future. As someone who was interested in their welfare and moral integrity.

7. As a caring grandmother always encouraging them to develop to their greatest potential.

8. As a valued friend who offers a little extra security beyond the immediate family circle.

9. As an independent person able to cope with aging and day-to-day problems but also a link with the older generation.

10. As one who was generous with her energy and talents.

"I should like to be remembered as a purveyor of laughter and fun, as an accepting person who tried to provide them with a haven of unconditional love and understanding."

Senior's Comments on the Delights of Grandparenting

The look of admiration and love as a grandchild sits on your lap is what being a senior is all about. If you have that and your health, you are indeed a fortunate person.

Harold Lemmon, Windsor

To be a senior is to have lots of the answers but nobody asks you the questions.

Louise Boddy, North York

It means that when my little granddaughter calls out loud, "Grandma knows best," I feel a bit proud.

Mabel Braidwood, Toronto

Today's delights are reflected in the merry eyes of a child, the comforting presence of a favourite animal, shadows of trees on sunlit snow, and a deeper appreciation of every new day.

Helen Owen, Bayfield

The one great delight seniors have is acquiring grandchildren. No one ever tells us what an unexpectedly magical pleasure there is in holding one's first grandchild.

Evelyn J. Broy, Windsor

(Culled from an issue of Ontario's splendid paper *Especially for Seniors*)

One final question for each of us to answer:

F) Have we as grandmothers succeeded in this demanding role?

One grandmother provided this short poem which may give us the answer:

To know that even one life breathed easier because you lived This is to have succeeded.

Bessie Anderson Stanley

Granny Locke by Charlie (age 3)
From Betty's Refridgerator Door Art Collection

Betty's Credentials:

♡ B.A. and High School Teaching Diploma
from McGill University

♡ 19 years of teaching (grades 1-11)
spread over the 30's, 40's, 60's and 70's

♡ 10 years of Sunday School Teaching

♡ 13 years of Brownie work — first as a leader,
then as a trainer of leaders at the Provincial,
Canadian and World levels

♡ 33 YEARS AS A GRANDMOTHER

♡ 1 YEAR AS A GREAT GRANDMOTHER

A Few Pages for Your Own Notes and Memories

♡

♡

A Few Pages for Your Own Notes and Memories

♡